presented to

Bj

from

Jill

date

Happy Birthday
2013

a lifetime of *Girlfriends*

moments of leisure

by Bonnie Jensen

BARBOUR
PUBLISHING

Bonnie would like to acknowledge the generous contribution of Anita Wiegand to this little book of friendship. She is not only a joy to work with, but a joy to befriend as well.

Scripture quotations marked TLB are taken from *The Living Bible* copyright © 1971. Used by permission of Tyndale House Publishers, Inc., Wheaton, Illinois 60189. All rights reserved.

Scripture quotations marked THE MESSAGE are taken from **THE MESSAGE**. Copyright © by Eugene H. Peterson 1993, 1994, 1995. Used by permission of NavPress Publishing Group.

Scripture quotations marked NIV are taken from the HOLY BIBLE, NEW INTERNATIONAL VERSION®. NIV®. Copyright © 1973, 1978, 1984 by International Bible Society. Used by permission of Zondervan Publishing House. All rights reserved.

Cover and interior images: Getty Images
Designed by Julie Doll.

Published by Barbour Publishing, Inc., P.O. Box 719, Uhrichsville, Ohio 44683, www.barbourbooks.com

Our mission is to publish and distribute inspirational products offering exceptional value and biblical encouragement to the masses.

 Member of the
Evangelical Christian
Publishers Association

Printed in China.
5 4 3 2 1

Leisure. . .simplicity. . .comfort. . .ease. . .
These are the joys and privileges
of seasoned friendships.

The best mirror is an old friend.

—George Herbert

Never abandon
a friend.

Proverbs 27:10 tlb

My friends are
my estate.
—Emily Dickinson

forever more

True friendship is a plant of
slow growth and must
undergo and withstand the
shocks of adversity before it is
entitled to the appellation.
—*George Washington*

lasting

beautiful

Life is filled with many beautiful
things. . . . Friendship is one of them.

loyal

A true friend is always loyal.

<small>PROVERBS 17:17 TLB</small>

It is great to have friends when one is young, but indeed it is still more so when you are getting old. When we are young, friends are, like everything else, a matter of course. In the old days we know what it means to have them.

—*Edvard Grieg*

I am wealthy in my friends.
—William Shakespeare

Good friends are
like a pair of shoes. . .
the longer you have
them, the more
comfortable the fit.

If I had a flower for every time a
friend has been a blessing in my life,
I'd have a bouquet big enough to fill
the month of May.

He wraps you in goodness—beauty
eternal. He renews your youth—
you're always young in his presence.

Psalm 103:5 The Message

O grant me, Heaven, a middle state,
Neither too humble nor too great;
More than enough, for nature's ends,
With something left to treat my friends.
—*David Mallet*

humble

Friendship is one thing
of beauty that never
fails to age gracefully.

graceful

happiness

Cherish all your happy moments; they
make a fine cushion for old age.
—*Booth Tarkington*

health

Dear friend, I pray that you may enjoy
good health and that all may go well
with you.

3 JOHN 1:2 NIV

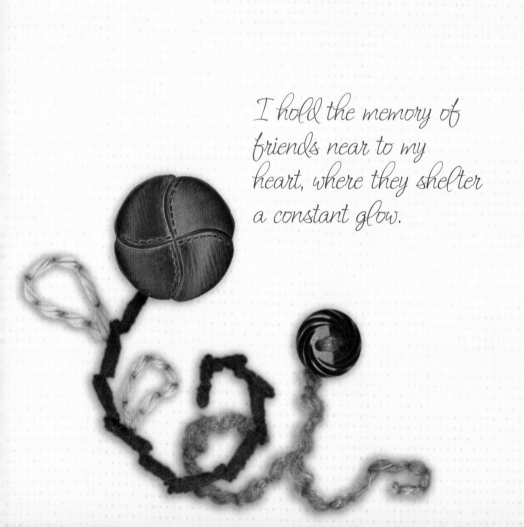

I hold the memory of
friends near to my
heart, where they shelter
a constant glow.

I thank God for all
things good—peace,
happiness, laughter, friends.

Be encouraged and knit together by strong ties of love.

COLOSSIANS 2:2 TLB

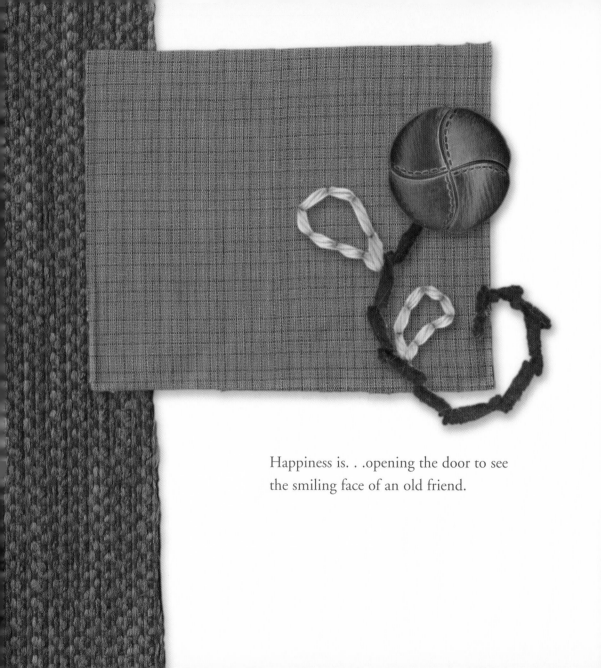

Happiness is. . .opening the door to see
the smiling face of an old friend.

No lapse of time or
distance of place can lessen
the friendship of those who
are truly persuaded of each
other's worth.

—Anonymous

Familiar faces have
a way of comforting
the soul.

familiar. . .

As a white candle
In a holy place,
So is the beauty
Of an aged face.
—*Joseph Campbell,*
"The Old Woman"

faces

youth

In a dream you are never eighty.
—*Anne Sexton, "Old"*

abundance

One friend in a lifetime is much; two are
many; three are hardly possible.
—*Henry Adams,*
The Education of Henry Adams

Grown up, and that is a terribly
hard thing to do. It is much easier
to skip it and go from one childhood
to another.
—*F. Scott Fitzgerald,* The Crack-Up

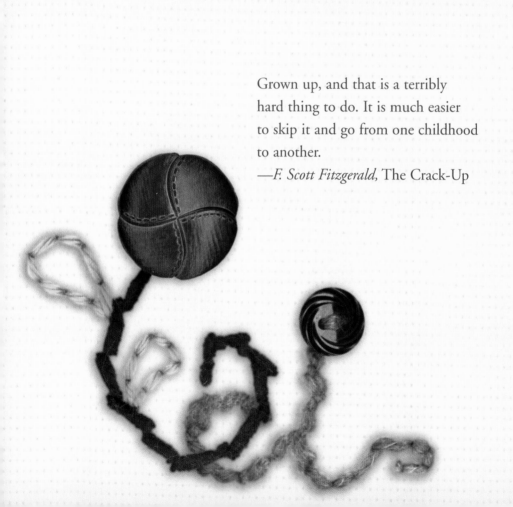

*A friendship that
lasts a lifetime is
as rare and precious
as a gem.*

Give yourself permission to be young again!

The language of friendship is not words,
but meanings.
  —*Henry David Thoreau*

True
friends
are part
of His
master
plan.

Think of a few friends who
have made a profound
impact on your life. . . .
Remember to thank them.

appreciation

I am who I am, in part,
because my life was
touched by the kindness
of friends.

Kindness

leisure

I joy to see myself now live: this age
best pleaseth me.

—*Robert Herrick*

reconnecting

Ah, how good it feels! The hand of an
old friend.

—*Henry Wadsworth Longfellow*

Five Wonderful Blessings of Age

You get to be silly and people
think you're cute.

You get to appreciate more,
remember less, and realize how
good they both can be.

You get to move slowly.

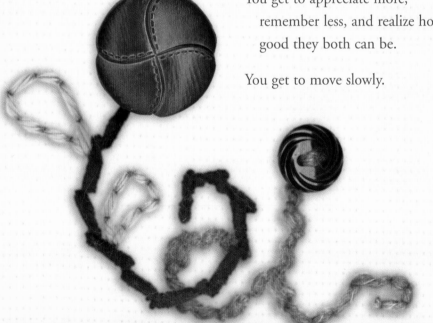

You get to see the world
through the eyes of wisdom.

You get to believe that your
life revolves around your
friends. . .and when you get to
see them again.

Old friends, new friends,
tried friends, true friends. . .
the comfort on which our
heart depends.

A grown woman's heart is full of memories—the sweetest of which are tied to friends.

Social Security
—the comfort
of knowing your
circle of friends
will be there for you.

*Laughter comes
easier with good
friends and more
often with old ones.*

Laughter

We can count on
a friend to teach
us gentle lessons.

lessons

guide

Have a grateful heart toward the friends who
have helped to guide you through life.

teach

You use steel to sharpen steel, and one
friend sharpens another.

PROVERBS 27:17 THE MESSAGE

There are a lot of ways to be a good friend. . .but to be an old one takes the precious gift of time.

I used to think my house had
to be in perfect order to
invite a friend to tea. Now I
realize we're both very happy
to be together in a dusty
house with warm cookies.

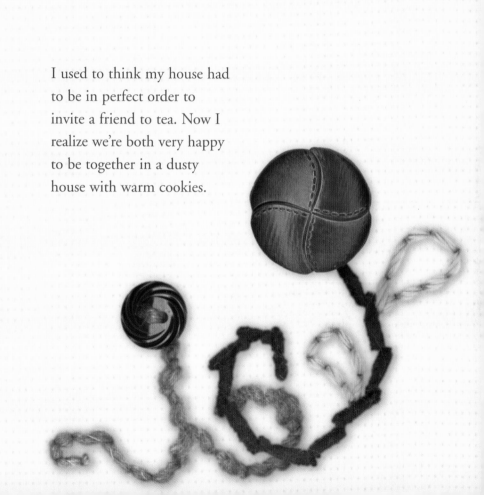

*Friends are
the best way to
fill memories
with laughter.*

To brag freely about children and grandchildren. . .
To laugh loudly over shared memories. . .
To relax completely in conversation. . .
These are the comforts and gifts of lifelong friendship.

Friendship:
the place
where trust
meets joy
and laughter
erases care.

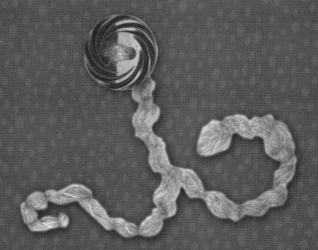

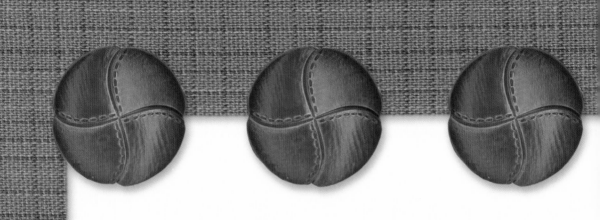

Lifelong friendship is
so rare, it should be
protected and cared for
as if nothing else in the
world could replace it.

lifelong

Friendship is the
blanket that wraps
around you on life's
coldest days.

comfort

advice

Perfume and incense bring joy to the heart,
and the pleasantness of one's friend springs
from his earnest counsel.

PROVERBS 27:9 NIV

giving

Friendship is giving—wholeheartedly. . .
sacrificially. . .lovingly.

God knew the seasons of life
would bring sunshine and rain. . .
for both He created the shelter
of friendship.

The lives that have been the
greatest blessing to you are the
lives of those people who
themselves were unaware of
having been a blessing.
—*Oswald Chambers*

In friendship it is never
really necessary to grow up;
it is essential, however, to
grow in our capacity to love.

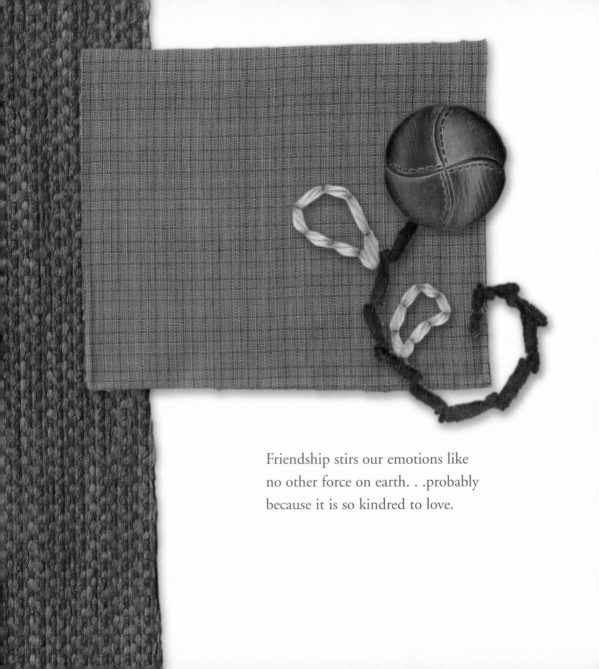

Friendship stirs our emotions like
no other force on earth. . .probably
because it is so kindred to love.

How in the world does anyone make
it through life without friends?
They're what color is to flowers. . .
warmth is to the sun. . .
and chocolate is to the taste buds.

The poignant moments in
my life almost always
involved my friends.
There were difficult times
when I "grew" a little in
my capacity to forgive,

forgiveness

happy times when I felt
most in touch with God's
joy, and sad times when
my heart swelled with
more compassion than I
thought was possible.

compassion

the best

Grow old along with me!
The best is yet to be.
—*Robert Browning*

precious

Treat a friend as you would fine lace
—as a delicate work of art.

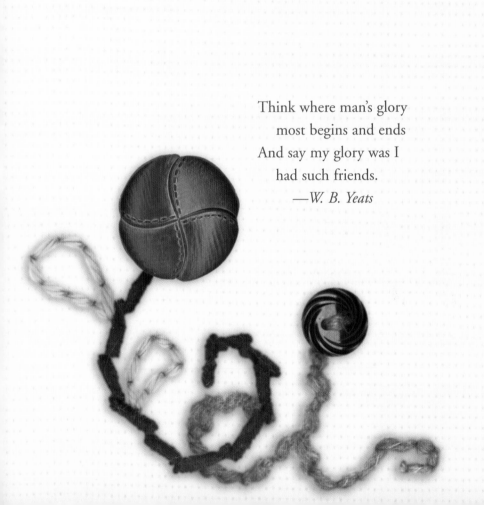

Think where man's glory
most begins and ends
And say my glory was I
had such friends.
—*W. B. Yeats*

A cheerful look brings joy to
the heart.
PROVERBS 15:30 NIV

After years of
walking together
through trials and
triumphs alike,
there is nothing
sweeter than hours
of leisure in the
company of friends.

The wrinkles of friendship are fine creases left by years of sharing tears and laughter—they are lines that add beauty and grace to this wonderful gift from God. . .reminding us of the journey we could not have traveled alone.

A friend should bear his friend's infirmities.
—*William Shakespeare*

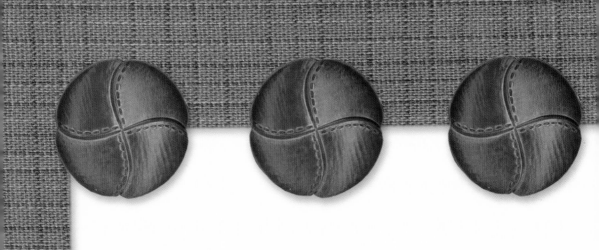

Friendship grows
eloquent with the
passing of years.

refinement

The family with an
old person in it
possesses a jewel.
—Chinese Proverb

sparkling

knowledge

Friendship has taught me a special skill.
Not only do I read between the lines, but I
can read between words, too, and all the
while decipher whether it is the heart or
the head that is speaking.

My life is
a journey
made beautiful
by friendship.

Friendship is like an
heirloom antique.
If it is aged and well
preserved, it is invaluable.

I hope that being silly with my friends never becomes a breach of good propriety—we'll be repeat offenders.

Hold a true friend with
both your hands.
—Nigerian Proverb

It's possible (and likely) that I have at least one friend who knows me better than I know myself. She has an amazing ability to bypass what I'm saying and go directly to what I'm thinking. It's both comforting and startling at the same time.

Macaroni and cheese. Hot
cocoa. Chicken noodle soup.
Old friends. These are the
comforts of a good life.

simple comforts

When your children are grown and on their own, you can once again find pleasure in simple joys, like spending time in your garden and strolling through the park. It's like taking a journey back to your childhood when simple pleasures were part of every day.

simple joys

faith

He'll make you young again! He'll take care
of you in old age.

RUTH 4:15 THE MESSAGE

character

If wrinkles indicate where smiles have been, at
one time or another my entire face, and a great
deal of my body, has grinned.

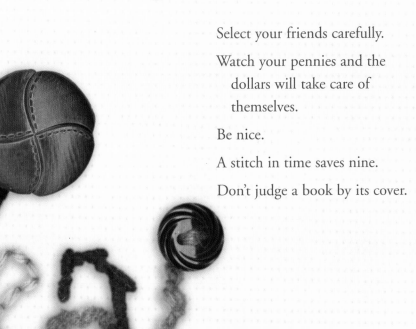

A Grandmother's Wisdom:

Select your friends carefully.

Watch your pennies and the
dollars will take care of
themselves.

Be nice.

A stitch in time saves nine.

Don't judge a book by its cover.

Mind your manners.

Keep your chin up.

Give your cares to God.

Mistakes will become the
   finest lessons.

Give cheerfully, love fully,
   forgive completely.

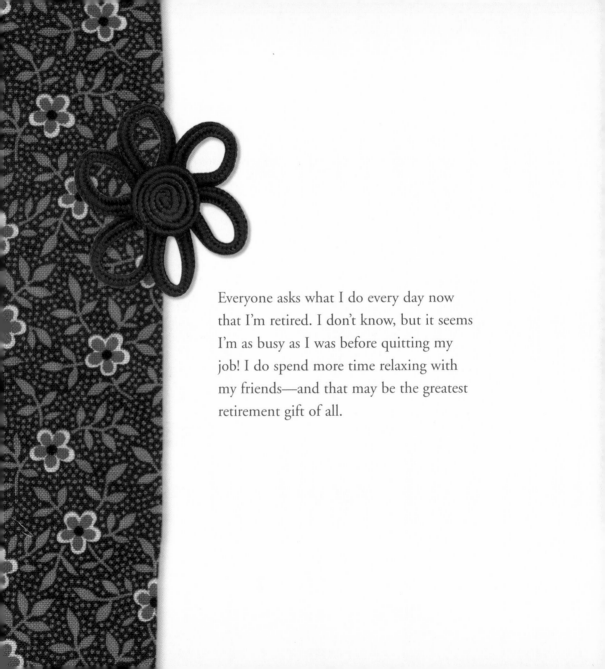

Everyone asks what I do every day now that I'm retired. I don't know, but it seems I'm as busy as I was before quitting my job! I do spend more time relaxing with my friends—and that may be the greatest retirement gift of all.

Fear less, hope more;
Eat less, chew more;
Whine less, breath more;
Talk less, say more;
Love more,
And all good things will be yours.
    —*Swedish Proverb*